HEATHCLIFF TRIPLE THREAT

The funniest feline in America delights millions of
fans every day as he appears in over 500 newspapers.
You'll have a laugh a minute as Heathcliff tangles with
the milkman, the fish store owner, the tuna fisherman
and just about everyone else he runs into. If you're
looking for some fun, look no further, Heathcliff is
here.

HEATHCLIFF

Triple Threat

by George Gately

CHARTER BOOKS, NEW YORK

HEATHCLIFF TRIPLE THREAT

A Charter Book / published by arrangement with
McNaught Syndicate, Inc.

PRINTING HISTORY
Sixteenth printing / December 1984

ISBN: 0-441-32215-8

Charter Books are published by The Berkley Publishing Group,
200 Madison Avenue, New York, New York 10016.
PRINTED IN THE UNITED STATES OF AMERICA

"DO YOU HAVE TO SWAT EVERYTHING THAT MOVES?!"

"LOOK OUT!...YOU'RE STANDING IN HEATHCLIFF'S CATNIP PATCH!"

"HE'S DEVELOPED GARBAGE DUMPING INTO A BALLET!!"

"SHE SOUNDS TERRIBLE TONIGHT!"

"HE'S BEEN SELLING ADVERTISING SPACE
ON SPIKE'S DOG HOUSE!"

"HE COMES DOWNTOWN EVERY DAY JUST TO BUG ME...
NOW HE'S EVEN JOINED A CAR POOL!!"

"I'M AFRAID THIS WON'T DO...SOMEONE OTHER THAN HEATHCLIFF HAS TO SIGN YOUR REPORT CARD!"

"HERE COMES AUNT MILDRED...THE ONE WHO GAVE HEATHCLIFF A PLASTIC SCRATCHING POST!"

"DON'T PICK ON THE GREAT BAZOOLI'S CAT ANYMORE!"

"ARE YOU GOING TO TIE UP THAT PHONE ALL DAY?!"

"WHENEVER YOU'RE FINISHED WITH THE
SUN TAN LOTION....."

"HE'S ORGANIZED A FISH FRY!"

"THEY'RE DINING FORMALLY THIS EVENING!"

"HE'LL BE HERE AS SOON AS THEY FINISH HIS MAKE-UP."

"THE SWORDFISH HAS BEEN ACTING RATHER JUMPY."

"WOULD YOU MIND ?!"

"BOY!... HE SURE GOT THE GOOD WOOD ON THAT ONE!"

"NOW MAYBE YOU'LL STOP PEEKING IN THE POTS
TO SEE WHAT'S COOKING!"

"HE HATES WATERMELON!"

"HE WANTS TO KNOW ABOUT HER DOWRY."

"...AND HERE TO CHRISTEN THE LATEST ADDITION TO THE TUNA FLEET...."

"NO, I HAVEN'T SEEN TODAY'S PAPER....WHY?"

"I WISH HE WOULDN'T DO THAT TO COLONEL BOTTLEWELL!!"

5-27

"ISN'T THAT SWEET ?!... HE'S FILLING THE BIRD BATH !"

"HE'S IN HERE, GRANDMA, GRILLING A MOUSE."

"WHERE'S OUR STEAM SHOVEL?"

"BY GOLLY!...COMES DINNER TIME AND AN ALARM MUST GO OFF IN YOUR STOMACH!"

"THANK YOU VERY MUCH."

"HE'S HERE, MRS. NUTMEG...HE JUST TURNED HIMSELF IN."

"GO FISH OFF THE DOCK LIKE EVERYONE ELSE!"

"HEATHCLIFF!...ARE YOU USING MY BOW AND ARROW?!"

"HAVE YOU SEEN HEATHCLIFF'S NEW BOP BAG?"

"HE PULLED THE OLD 'SHADOW-ON-THE-WALL' TRICK AGAIN!"

"I NEVER KNEW HE HAD A SISTER!"

"IT'S ONLY FOR CHUBBY LADIES."

"WHAT METER MAN?!...THE METER MAN
WAS HERE YESTERDAY!"

"I DIDN'T PUT ANY GARBAGE OUT BECAUSE
WE WERE ON VACATION!"

"SOMEONE KEEPS HISSING!"

"NEVER TOUCH HIS TEDDY BEAR!"

"HE TANGLED WITH A SKUNK!"

"THERE'S SOMEONE HERE ABOUT A DISH OF CAT FOOD!"

"WHAT HAVE YOU DONE NOW?!"

"COME BACK HERE WITH OUR GIANT CLAM!"

"YOU GAVE THAT SHEEPDOG AN AWFUL FRIGHT!"

"THE JUDGE IS OVER THERE, TALKING TO
HEATHCLIFF'S PRESS AGENT."

"NO!...YOU CAN'T HAVE A TABLE!!"

"I THINK THEY'D LIKE TO NEGOTIATE!"

"IT WAS DUMPED OVER BY A TINY INFANT!"

"NO TICKET!"

"HE'S MAKING HIMSELF A TOSSED TUNA SALAD."

"WHO ASKED FOR *YOUR* OPINION ?!"

"MARCH YOURSELF RIGHT OUT OF HERE
WITH THAT HARPOON!"

"DO WE JUDGE THEM ON SOCIAL GRACES ?!"

"HE'S PRACTICING HIS PLACE KICKING."

"I GET A LOT OF MY INFORMATION FROM
SECRET AGENT DOUBLE "O" HEATHCLIFF!"

"YOU WERE SUPPOSED TO HAVE HER HOME
BY TWELVE O'CLOCK!"

"THAT IS NOT A BACK SCRATCHER!....
THAT'S AN ELECTRIC TOOTHBRUSH!!"

"I DON'T THINK THEY HAVE A GARBAGE CAN
DUMPING EVENT IN THE OLYMPICS!"

"BETTER TAKE THAT MEGAPHONE AWAY FROM OUR MASCOT!"

"OKAY....YOU KEEP RIPPING THEM UP AND
I'LL KEEP WRITING THEM!"

"TONIGHT MUST BE AMATEUR NIGHT!"

"YOUR CLEANING LADY IS HERE."

"NOW, THERE'S A REAL STUPID MOUSE!!"

"JUST LOOK AT YOUR CARRIAGE!...IT'S A MESS!"

"HE PLEADS INNOCENT ON ALL SEVENTY-FOUR COUNTS!"

" HERE WE HAVE EXHIBIT 'A'...."

"WELL, YOU BEAT THE RAP ONCE AGAIN!"

"TARZAN AND JANE!"

"I'LL GIVE YOU A HERRING IF YOU'LL GO AWAY!"

"WHAT HAVE YOU DONE TO SPIKE'S DOG LICENSE ?!"

"DON'T DO IT, FELLA!...HEATHCLIFF CONTROLS ALL GARBAGE CANS ON THE ENTIRE EAST SIDE OF TOWN!"

"DON'T KILL IT!...IT'S ONE OF MY EYELASHES!"

"IT'S NO USE TRYING TO TALK TO HIM!"

"WE HAVE ENOUGH CHEERLEADERS."

"MAN.!—HE IS DEADLY WITH THAT SCRATCHING POST!"

"HE'S REGISTERED RIGHT HERE...HEATHCLIFF NUTMEG!"

"EXCUSE ME, SIR...WHERE DOES HE REPORT
TO HIS PAROLE OFFICER?"

"HEATHCLIFF IS GETTING RESTLESS."

"THEY'LL HAVE TO KICK THAT ONE AGAIN, FOLKS!"

"WE HAVE **OUR OWN** HALFTIME FESTIVITIES PLANNED, IF YOU DON'T MIND!"

"THAT'S HIS FAVORITE TV SHOW!"

"IT'S SPIKE'S SISTER."

"YOU SHOULDN'T HAVE TOUCHED THAT ONE, MISTER...THAT'S *HIS* TREE!"

"I'VE BEEN SEARCHING EVERYWHERE FOR THAT GIRDLE!"

"HE LIKES TO FATTEN THEM UP!"

"DOWN, FANG!...THERE'S NO NEED TO STAND AND SALUTE!"

"KNOCK, KNOCK!"

"SITTING IN FOR HEATHCLIFF TONIGHT IS HIS GUEST HOST, TABBY McCLOSKY!"

"DOES HE *HAVE* TO DRINK HIS MILK FROM A BRANDY SNIFTER?!"

"I UNDERSTAND HE WAS
IN A CAT FIGHT."

"OH-OH!... GOOD EVENING, COUNT DRACULA!"

"HEATHCLIFF'S TEACHING SPIKE NOT TO CHASE CARS."